The Missions: California's Heritage

MISSION SANTA INÉS

by

Mary Null Boulé

Merryant Publishing
Vashon, Washington

Book Nineteen in a series of twenty-one

With special thanks to Msgr. Francis J. Weber, Archivist of the Los Angeles Catholic Diocese for his encouragement and expertise in developing this series.

Father Junípero Serra

INTRODUCTION

Building of a mission church involved everyone in the mission community. Priests were engineers and architects; Native Americans did the construction. Mission Indian in front is pouring adobe mix into a brick form. Bricks were then dried in the sun.

FATHER SERRA AND THE MISSIONS: AN INTRODUCTION

The year was 1769. On the east coast of what would soon become the United States, the thirteen original colonies were making ready to break away from England. On the west coast of our continent, however, there could be found only untamed land inhabited by Native Americans, or Indians. Although European explorers had sailed up and down the coast in their ships, no one but American Indians had explored the length of this land on foot . . . until now.

To this wild, beautiful country came a group of adventurous men from New Spain, as Mexico was then called. They were following the orders of their king, King Charles III of Spain.

One of the men was a Spanish missionary named Fray Junípero Serra. He had been given a tremendous job; especially since he was fifty-six years old, an old man in those days. King Charles III had ordered mission settlements to be built along the coast of Alta (Upper) California and it was Fr. Serra's task to carry out the king's wishes.

Father Serra had been born in the tiny village of Petra

on the island of Mallorca, Spain. He had done such an excellent job of teaching and working with the Indians in Mexican missions, the governor of New Spain had suggested to the king that Fr. Serra do the same with the Indians of Alta California. Hard-working Fray Serra was helped by Don Gaspár de Portolá, newly chosen governor of Alta California, and two other Franciscan priests who had grown up with Fr. Serra in Mallorca, Father Fermin Lasuén and Father Francisco Palóu.

There were several reasons why men had been told to build settlements along the coast of this unexplored country. First, missions would help keep the land as Spanish territory. Spain wanted to be sure the rest of the world knew it owned this rich land. Second, missions were to be built near harbors so towns would grow there. Ships from other countries could then stop to trade with the Spaniards, but these travelers could not try to claim the land for themselves. Third, missions were a good way to turn Indians into Christian, hard-working people.

It would be nice if we could write here that everything went well; that twenty-one missions immediately sprang up along the coast. Unfortunately, all did not go well. It would take fifty-four years to build all the California missions. During those fifty-four years many people died from Indian attacks, sickness, and starvation. Earthquakes and fires constantly ruined mission buildings, which then had to be built all over again. Fr. Serra calmly overcame each problem as it happened, as did those priests who followed him.

When a weary Fray Serra finally died in 1784, he had founded nine missions from San Diego to Monterey and had arranged the building of many more. Fr. Lasuén continued Fr. Serra's work, adding eight more missions to the California mission chain. The remaining four missions were founded in later years.

Originally, plans had been to place missions a hard day's walk from each other. Many of them were really quite far apart. Travelers truly struggled to go from one mission to another along the 650 miles of walking road known as El Camino Real, The Royal Highway. Today keen eyes will sometimes see tall, curved poles with bells hanging from them sitting by the side of streets and highways. These bell poles are marking a part of the old El Camino Real.

At first Spanish soldiers were put in charge of the towns which grew up near each mission. The priests were told to handle only the mission and its properties. It did not take long to realize the soldiers were not kind and gentle leaders. Many were uneducated and did not have the understanding they should have had in dealing with people. So the padres came to be in charge of not only the mission, but of the townspeople and even of the soldiers.

The first missions at San Diego and Monterey were built near the ocean where ships could bring them needed supplies. After early missions began to grow their own food and care for themselves, later mission compounds were built farther away from the coast. What one mission did well, such as leatherworking, candlemaking, or raising cattle, was shared with other missions. As a result, missions became somewhat specialized in certain products.

Although mission buildings looked different from mission to mission, most were built from one basic plan. Usually a compound was constructed as a large, four-sided building with an inner patio in the center. The outside of the quadrangle had only one or two doors, which were locked at night to protect the mission. A church usually sat at one corner of the quadrangle and was always the tallest and largest part of the mission compound.

Facing the inner patio were rooms for the two priests living there, workshops, a kitchen, storage rooms for grain and food, and the mission office. Rooms along the back of the quadrangle often served as home to the unmarried Indian women who worked in the kitchen. The rest of the Indians lived just outside the walls of the mission in their own village.

Beyond the mission wall and next to the church was a cemetery. Today you can still see many of the original headstones of those who died while living and working at the mission. Also outside the walls were larger workshops, a reservoir holding water used at the mission, and orchards containing fruit trees. Huge fields surrounded each mission where crops grew and livestock such as sheep, cattle, and horses grazed.

It took a great deal of time for some Indian tribes to understand the new way of life a mission offered, even though the

Native Americans always had food and shelter when they became mission Indians. Each morning all Indians were awakened at sunrise by a church bell calling them to church. Breakfast followed church . . . and then work. The women spun thread and made clothes, as well as cooked meals. Men and older boys worked in workshops or fields and constructed buildings. Meanwhile the Indian children went to school, where the padres taught them. After a noon meal there was a two hour rest before work began again. After dinner the Indians sang, played, or danced. This way of life was an enormous change from the less organized Indian life before the missionaries arrived. Many tribes accepted the change, some had more trouble getting used to a regular schedule, some tribes never became a part of mission life.

Water was all-important to the missions. It was needed to irrigate crops and to provide for the mission people and animals. Priests designed and engineered magnificent irrigation systems at most of the missions. All building of aqueducts and reservoirs of these systems was done by the mission Indians.

With all the organized hard work, the missions did very well. They grew and became strong. Excellent vineyards gave wine for the priests to use and to sell. Mission fields produced large grain crops of wheat and corn, and vast grazing land developed huge herds of cattle and sheep. Mission life was successful for over fifty years.

When Mexico broke away from Spain, it found it did not have enough money to support the California missions, as Spain had been doing. So in 1834, Mexico enforced the secularization law which their government had decreed several years earlier. This law stated missions were to be taken away from the missionaries and given to the Indians. The law said that if an Indian did not want the land or buildings, the property was to be sold to anyone who wished to buy it.

It is true the missions had become quite large and powerful. And as shocked as the padres were to learn of the secularization law, they also knew the missions had originally been planned as temporary, or short term projects. The priests had been sure their Indians would be well-trained enough to run the missions by themselves when the time came to move to other unsettled lands. In fact, however, even after fifty years the California Indians were still not ready to handle the huge missions.

Since the Indians did not wish to continue the missions, the buildings and land were sold, the Indians not even waiting for money or, in some cases, receiving money for the sale.

Sad times lay ahead. Many Indians went back to the old way of life. Some Indians stayed on as servants to the new owners and often these owners were not good to them. Mission buildings were used for everything from stores and saloons to animal barns. In one mission the church became a barracks for the army. A balcony was built for soldiers with their horses stabled in the altar area. Rats ate the stored grain and beautiful church robes. Furniture and objects left by the padres were stolen. People even stole the mission building roof tiles, which then caused the adobe brick walls to melt from rain. Earthquakes finished off many buildings.

Shortly after California became a part of the United States in the mid-1860s, our government returned all mission buildings to the Catholic Church. By this time most of them were in terrible condition. Since the priests needed only the church itself and a few rooms to live in, the other rooms of the mission were rented to anyone who needed them. Strange uses were found in some cases. In the San Fernando Mission, for example, there was once a pig farm in the patio area.

Tourists finally began to notice the mission ruins in the early 1900s. Groups of interested people got together to see if the missions could be restored. Some missions had been "modernized" by this time, unfortunately, but within the last thirty years historians have found enough pictures, drawings, and written descriptions to rebuild or restore most of the missions to their original appearances.

The restoration of all twenty-one missions is a splendid way to preserve our California heritage. It is the hope of many Californians that this dream of restoration can become a reality in the near future.

MISSION SANTA INÉS

I. THE MISSION TODAY

Mission Santa Inés is located on the eastern edge of the town of Solvang. It sits on a ridge overlooking the rich Santa Ynez Valley. As you stand in front of the well-kept mission and look down the valley you can see the old mission grist mill nearly four miles away. As unspoiled as the still valley is, you could easily imagine the year as 1820, and see yourself as a part of old mission life, rather than of our twentieth century.

The church, part of the convento, and the gardens are all that remain of the original quadrangle. These have been well-restored. You can see in your mind just how large the quadrangle was in mission days when you look at the remains of the nineteenth arch of the original twenty-two arches. It stands alone almost a city block away from the present day convento with its nine restored arches. The roof of the corridor forms a balcony to the second story of the convento. This balcony was completely roofed over for more than 100 years. No one realized the convento had two stories until restoration began in 1947!

Inside the convento is a gift shop and a very well-organized museum with collections of objects from mission life. Between the museum and the church is a twelve-foot-thick wall into which a doorway has been cut as an entrance to the church proper. One can tell that Mission Santa Inés has an active church today. There is a warm feeling you get as you enter the building. Candles glow and prayer books are in the pews. The reredos, painted by the mission Indians in 1825, is done in fresco-style. It is still colorful after all these years. Fresco is the name given to designs painted on the adobe walls by the Indians. Native dyes of red, clay, green and gold were used.

The original statue of Saint Agnes, patroness saint of the mission, sits above the altar in a large niche in the center of the reredos. It is carved of wood, polychromed (painted), and came from Mexico in the early 1800s. It was partly restored in 1953.

Along the walls are the Fourteen Stations of the Cross. These oil paintings were painted in the late 1700s, and were copies of some old Italian woodcuts. The ceiling has its original beams and the floor tiles are also original. Even the original baptismal font made of hand-hammered zinc and copper is still in the small baptistry.

The outside of the church is quite plain. The only decoration is a small cross over the main entrance. Large wooden entrance doors are carved in the River of Life design, a pattern often used by the missionary priests long ago. An arched window is above the entrance. The church and convento are painted a light tan color trimmed in dark brown.

Attached to the church and opposite the convento is the restored campanario, or bell wall. It holds three of the original bells. They hang from arched openings and were made for Mission Santa Inés in Peru in 1807, 1817, and 1818.

Behind the campanario is the cemetery looking much as it always has, with wooden crosses marking the graves of some of the 1,600 Indians buried there.

Behind the convento is the beautifully-tended patio with its gardens and grape arbors. In the center of the patio is a fountain. An interesting piece of historic wall still stands at one side of the patio. It is built of stone and adobe mortar and came into being in 1836, when Mexican mayordomos were sent to manage the missions. This wall divided the mission into two areas; one for the manager and his family, and the other area, which included the church, for the padres, or priests.

The Capuchin Francescan Fathers take excellent care of the mission today.

II. HISTORY OF THE MISSION

Father Estévan Tapis founded Mission Santa Inés on September 17, 1804. He had high hopes for the success of Santa Inés because a mission was truly needed in this area. Mission Santa Bárbara and Mission La Purisima were much too far apart.

There were so many Chumash Indians nearby who wished to become a part of mission life, that a new mission would solve crowding problems at both Santa Bárbara and La Purisima. Furthermore, there was the hope that a mission here would make the warlike tribes of the Tulare Indians less trouble for the mission Indians.

But the truth is Santa Inés never became as large and successful as the missions around it. In fact, it was a working mission for only thirty-two years and never had as many Native Americans living there as lived in surrounding missions.

The first two priests put in charge, Fathers Gutierrez and Calzada, had such grand dreams for the mission they built a huge quadrangle which measured 350 feet on each side. Since the founding of Santa Inés was at a time when all the missions were doing very well, this new mission received a great deal of help from the rest of the missions and grew rapidly. It became famous for the beautiful leather saddles and iron and silver craftworks made in its workshops.

By 1812 many adobe brick workshops, storerooms, and rooms for soldiers had been completed. But already there was trouble at the mission. Mexico had stopped sending money to take care of the soldiers because it was in the middle of a revolution with Spain. The soldiers had to depend on the mission for food, clothing, and Indian help. The Indians disliked working for the soldiers for they were not as kind as the priests. In spite of all the trouble with the soldiers, however, the mission buildings continued to be built.

There was a terrible series of earthquakes that same year, just as the mission buildings were almost complete. A large part of the church and most of the other buildings were destroyed. The next five years were spent rebuilding the mission once again. A new, permanent church, the one seen today, was dedicated on July 4, 1817. It was 139 feet long and 26 feet wide. The walls were built of adobe and brick and varied in thickness from five to six feet. The ceiling beams were sugar pine brought from mountains thirty miles away. The roof was tiled.

It was during this time of rebuilding that Santa Inés had the most Indians, 768, living at the mission. Records show there were also 6,000 head of cattle; 5,000 sheep; 120 goats; 150

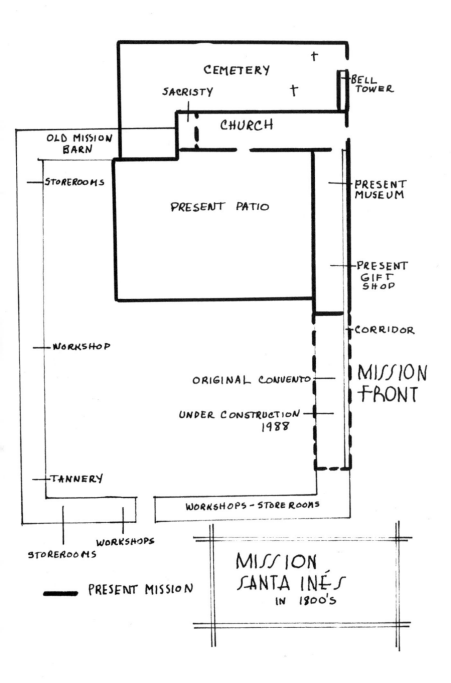

CEMETERY

BELL
TOWER

SACRISTY

CHURCH

OLD MISSION
BARN

STOREROOMS

PRESENT
MUSEUM

PRESENT PATIO

PRESENT
GIFT
SHOP

CORRIDOR

WORKSHOP

ORIGINAL CONVENTO

MISSION
FRONT

UNDER CONSTRUCTION
1988

TANNERY

WORKSHOPS - STOREROOMS

STOREROOMS

WORKSHOPS

PRESENT MISSION

MISSION
SANTA INÉS
IN 1800's

pigs; 120 pack mules; and 770 horses at the mission in 1817. Strangely, the crops and number of animals continued to grow larger after 1817, but the number of natives only grew less.

Finally, in 1824, the Indians became so angry at the soldiers they revolted. They set fire to the mission buildings and only when the church roof caught fire did the Indians realize what they were doing. It was the soldiers they hated, not the priest, Fr. Uria. The Indians themselves put out the church fire, but by this time all the workshops, the soldiers' houses, and the guardhouse had been burned to the ground. Once again the mission was rebuilt, over an eight year period, but never again was Mission Santa Inés to be a working mission.

In 1834, secularization was put into effect. The priests no longer could run the missions. The first person Mexico sent to be in charge of Santa Inés rented half of the mission for $580 a year. The priests were allowed only the convento and the church for their needs. The Indians disliked their new master and left the mission. With no one to care for the crops and the animals, the mission went to ruin.

In 1843, a seminary, a training center for priests, was begun at Santa Inés, but it soon moved to a new place. Then, in 1846, the Mexican governor of California, Señor Pio Pico, sold the mission to renters living there for $7,000. A few months later the United States took possession of California and gave some of the land and the mission itself back to the Catholic Church. Sadly, the church had no money to keep things in good repair, and the church building was in such bad condition that one Sunday the pulpit collapsed as a poor priest was speaking from it. The wood in the pulpit was too rotten to even rebuild it. A family named Donahue moved into one end of what was left of the convento in 1882. They lived there for sixteen years, trying their best to repair the building, but parts of the mission continued to fall apart.

Then, in 1904, Father Buckler came to take charge of Santa Inés. He began the first true effort to restore the mission. He re-roofed the church and what was left of the convento. He reinforced church walls and foundations and built a new water and drainage system. With the help of his niece he began the present-day museum. While he was in the middle of restoring, the campanario collapsed in a rainstorm in 1911. Instead of building a bell wall like the original, he built a new one in a completely different style. It was not until 1948 that a concrete bell tower built like the original replaced the flimsy wooden and plaster one built by Fr. Buckler.

When Fr. Buckler retired in 1924, the Capuchin Francescan (Irish) priests arrived to care for the mission. They installed electricity and indoor plumbing. However, it was not until help came from the Hearst Foundation in 1947, that major restoration began. Original floor tiles were uncovered, blocked-up doorways were opened, museum rooms were repaired, and special cases were built in the museum to show mission objects of interest. Some side altars which had been put in the church in the late 1800s were removed at that time.

In 1972 more restoration was completed and the outside of the mission was painted. Recently historically interesting areas of the mission grounds, such as the reservoir in front of the church, and the lavenderia (the Indian women's laundry basin), have been marked. Markers now point to the distant grist mill built in 1820.

The mission fathers hope restoration can continue until the entire convento with its twenty-two arches has been restored. As this book is being printed Mission Santa Inés is just beginning to rebuild most of the remainder of the original convento. Soon the grassy space between the first ten corridor arches and the lonely nineteenth arch will be filled with an extension to the present-day convento. All of the money for this restoration has been earned by the mission church and busy gift shop. Good for Mission Santa Inés!

Mainly pale green in color, reredos has been repainted often, but still looks almost as it did in mission times.

Patio behind remaining L of quadrangle. A piece of wall that once divided patio, when Mexican majordomos were sent to take charge of missions in 1830's, can be seen in foreground.

OUTLINE OF SANTA INÉS

I. The mission today

A. Location
  1. Town
  2. Valley
B. Convento
  1. Number of arches today
  2. Original arches
  3. Balcony and second story uncovered
  4. Museum and gift shop
     a. Twelve foot thick wall
C. Church interior
  1. Reredos
  2. Statue of St. Agnes
  3. Stations of the Cross
  4. Ceiling and floor
  5. Baptismal font
D. Church exterior
  1. Simple decoration
  2. Door design
  3. Color and trim
E. Campanario
  1. Age and number of bells
F. Cemetery
  1. Number of Indians buried there
G. Patio
  1. Gardens and grape arbors
  2. Fountain
  3. Historic wall

II. History of the mission

A. Founding date and priest
B. Need for mission
C. Success of mission
D. Building of mission
  1. Priests in charge
  2. Help from other missions
  3. Size of quadrangle

Outline continued next page

E. Mission completed 1812
   1. Famous for leather and metal works
   2. Troubles with Indians
      a. Soldiers treatment of Indians
   3. Earthquakes
      a. Rebuilding time
F. 1817
   1. Present day church dedication
      a. Size of church (and description)
   2. Success of mission at this time
G. Continued growth of crops and animals
   1. Indian population's growth?
H. Revolt of 1824
   1. Burning of buildings
I. End of working mission
J. Secularization
   1. Sharing of mission
   2. Mayordomo
   3. Indians leave
K. Mission sold
   1. Governor Pico
   2. United States returns mission to Catholic Church
L. Donahue family
   1. Care given church
M. Father Buckler
   1. Restoration begun
   2. Museum begun
   3. Church repairs
   4. Water system
   5. Rebuilt campanario
N. Capuchin Francescans
   1. Electricity and plumbing
O. Major restoration
   1. Hearst Foundation - 1947
P. Restoration from 1972 on
   1. Markers placed
Q. Priests' dreams

GLOSSARY

BUTTRESS: a large mass of stone or wood used to strengthen buildings

CAMPANARIO: a wall which holds bells

CLOISTER: an enclosed area; a word often used instead of convento

CONVENTO: mission building where priests lived

CORRIDOR: covered, outside hallway found at most missions

EL CAMINO REAL: highway between missions; also known as The King's Highway

FACADE: front wall of a building

FONT: large, often decorated bowl containing Holy Water for baptizing people

FOUNDATION: base of a building, part of which is below the ground

FRESCO: designs painted directly on walls or ceilings

LEGEND: a story coming from the past

PORTICO: porch or covered outside hallway

PRESERVE: to keep in good condition without change

PRESIDIO: a settlement of military men

QUADRANGLE: four-sided shape; the shape of most missions

RANCHOS: large ranches often many miles from mission proper where crops were grown and animal herds grazed

REBUILD: to build again; to repair a great deal of something

REPLICA: a close copy of the original

REREDOS: the wall behind the main altar inside the church

*RESTORATION: to bring something back to its original condition (see * below)

SANCTUARY: area inside, at the front of the church where the main altar is found

SECULARIZATION: something not religious; a law in mission days taking the mission buildings away from the church and placing them under government rule

*ORIGINAL: the first one; the first one built

BIBLIOGRAPHY

Bauer, Helen. *California Mission Days.* Sacramento, CA: California State Department of Education, 1957.

Goodman, Marian. *Missions of California.* Redwood City, CA: Redwood City Tribune, 1962.

Merrill, King. *Old Mission Santa Inés.* No location: Viking Press, no date.

Sunset Editors. *The California Missions.* Menlo Park, CA: Lane Publishing Company, 1979.

Wright, Ralph B., ed. *California Missions.* Arroyo Grande, CA 93420: Hubert A. Lowman, 1977.

For more information about this mission, write to:

Old Mission Santa Inés
Solvang, CA 93463

It is best to enclose a self-addressed, stamped envelope and a small amount of money to pay for brochures and pictures the mission might send you.

CREDITS

Cover art and Father Serra Illustration: Ellen Grim
Illustrations: Alfredo de Batuc
Ground Layout: Mary Boulé